Year of the Snake

CRAB ORCHARD AWARD SERIES IN POETRY

T0288086

Year of the Snake

LEE ANN RORIPAUGH

Crab Orchard Review

Southern Illinois University Press

CARBONDALE

Printed in the United States of America

23   22   21   20   9   8   7   6

The Crab Orchard Award Series in Poetry is a joint publishing
venture of Southern Illinois University Press and *Crab Orchard Review*. This
series has been made possible by the generous support of the
Office of the President of Southern Illinois University and the Office
of the Vice Chancellor for Academic Affairs and Provost at Southern Illinois
University Carbondale.

Crab Orchard Award Series in Poetry Editor: Jon Tribble
Judge for 2003: Ralph Burns

Library of Congress Cataloging-in-Publication Data

Roripaugh, Lee Ann.
  Year of the snake / Lee Ann Roripaugh.
    p. cm. — (Crab Orchard award series in poetry)
  I. Title. II. Series.
PS3568.O717 Y43 2004
811'.54—dc22
ISBN 0-8093-2569-1 (pbk. : alk. paper)   2003016977

Printed on recycled paper. ♻

Contents

Acknowledgments

Poems in this book or excerpts have appeared or are forthcoming in the following journals:

Briar Cliff Review—"Loneliness"

Michigan Quarterly Review—"Snake Wife"

North American Review—"DDT" and "Octopus in the Freezer"

Parnassus: Poetry in Review—"Dream Carp"

Ploughshares—"Hope" and "Toothpick Warriors"

Prairie Schooner—"Antelope Jerky" and "Nanking Cherry Jam"

Puerto del Sol—"Girl with a Bowl on Her Head"

Quarterly West—"Happy Hour" and "Snake Song" (originally published under the title "Year of the Snake")

South Dakota Review—"Ennui," "Innocence," "Instinct," and "Nostalgia"

Sow's Ear Poetry Review—"Transience"

"Transplanting" was published in *Poets of the New Century,* edited by Rick Higgerson and Roger Weingarten (David R. Godine Publisher, 2001).

"Dream Carp," "Hope," and "Transplanting" were reprinted in *Asian American Poetry: The Next Generation,* edited by Victoria Chang (University of Illinois Press, 2003).

"Octopus in the Freezer" was reprinted in *Contemporary American Poetry: Behind the Scenes,* edited by Ryan G. Van Cleave (Allyn & Bacon/Longman, 2004).

Year of the Snake

Snake Song

I was born in the year of the snake
and maybe this is why
I speak with a forked tongue. I've followed

the vague sibilant thread
of the voice in my head curling
into a tangled snarl

of roots, grass, stems and leaves, so that when
I open my mouth to talk,
a strange song, not mine, comes tumbling out.

Ai-noko, half-caste, I tilt
my head in the mirror first this way
then that—Horikoshi

cheekbones, Caucasian nose, my *ojii-san*'s
serious eyebrows
feathering like ink strokes over eyes

not quite green, not quite brown,
in the tranquil white moon of my face.
My blood runs hot and cold.

Slit me open, let me pare away
my body's tourniquet
rind. Itch, twist and tug, I know the lust

for heavy glistening
coil wrapping itself around reborn
coil. I know the dangers

of the in-between. And so I keep
my skins as transient
as the inner tissue-paper wings

that ladybugs conceal
beneath the spotted shields of their bright
metallic shells. And then

I shed them, one after another,
like the discarded husks
of mayflies clinging in tenacious

rows to my window screens
in the summer, their hollowed sheaths
pearlescent—translucent

paned scales and two silver wisps of tail.
And when wind's warm breath comes
to unlock this instinctive gripping,

my ghost selves are carried
up like tiny dragon kites spiraling
higher, higher . . . higher.

Innocence

My parents wrapped an old sheet
around the playpen to shield me
from the television, but I learned
to pull up the edge and peer out
from underneath to see newsreels
from Vietnam. I remember stretchers,
helicopters, and trees flickering
sadness, ominous black and white.
But the night of the moon landing
I was given my dinner early
then plucked from slumber, flushed
and cranky, wrapped in a crocheted
afghan and propped up on the sofa
in front of Walter Cronkite.
I was four, and secretly I wondered
if I would see the moon rabbit,
who was pulled from flame and taken
to live in the sky by the old man
in the moon. But instead there was
crackling static, the disembodied
voices of the astronauts, chubby
in their white spacesuits
as they finally climbed down
the ladder to bob on the rocky
surface of the moon as if it were
elastic as a trampoline. So quiet
and dark, it seemed lonelier
than Wyoming when snow spilled
over the fence tops and made strange
bent shapes of the Russian olive
and pine trees, hulking silent

humps of the cars, and antelope
stepped into the frozen circle
of the city limits. I became
a child of the moon landing—
raised on Tang and Pillsbury space
food sticks, chewy in the silver-
lined, tubular wrappers—my face
tilted up like a stargazer lily,
with its red-tipped matchstick
stamens yearning, antennae-like,
for the Sea of Tranquility, the void
beyond. At night I watched the man
who lived in the house across
the back alley from my bedroom
walk around without his clothes
through my pirate's telescope.
And when I was tired of watching him
I watched the moon instead, hanging
pale orange, like a melon-balled
scoop of cantaloupe in the sky.
Empty, shimmering rock-cold fruit,
but I wanted to swallow it whole.

Love Potion

My mother's plants
are like favored siblings. She cuts
back their stalks, nips

their buds with quick, ruthless snips. They grow,
bloom, and don't talk
back. I become good at sabotage—

tearing the heads
off snapdragons, pinching open
their jaws between

thumb and forefinger to stare down
their gaping throats—
pistil and stamen ivory wisps

of uvula,
flickering tongue. I stuff each one
of their mouths with

the juicy, choking weight of a
Nanking cherry,
and line their heads in colored rows

along the back
alley fence as a warning.
I steal an old

margarine tub, the kind with
orange crowns, fill it
with pink drops of my mother's hand

lotion, a shot
of Chanel No. 5, then stir
in crushed mint leaves,

the tender petals of sweet peas,
four spider legs
pulled from the Daddy Longlegs caught

lurking around
the back door, the yellow, pinhead
centers of my

mother's African violets,
which roll about
like plucked-out insect eyes. A squirt

of sour rhubarb
juice, a creamy dab of Pond's cold
cream, and a spritz

of mosquito repellent for
good measure. Next
I gather Siberian snow

peas from the
caragana bushes that border
the side fence, slit

open the slim pods at the seams
with a red-stained
thumbnail to spill out a palm

full of peas, pale
green, like tiny lima beans, to
string together

with dental floss and a needle.
I wait three days
for the peas to turn hard and round

and brown, with tor-
toise shell whorls like tiger's-eye beads,
and then I drape

the necklace as an offering
around the bony
clavicles, the fierce pear-shaped breasts

of the South Seas
wooden carving my mother hides
behind large pots

of Christmas cactus, whose earlobes
I like to rub for luck.
I let the love potion ripen,

grow swollen, rank
and full of power, and then I dab
it, like ointment,

inside the sleeve of my mother's
pillowcase, on
the cuffs of her denim jacket,

along the brim
of her gardening hat, a dotted
trail on the face

of her hand mirror. I think that
her heart is made
of glass, that my fingerprints will

sour, and flake off
like dried milk. But instead, I find
her in the garden,

cross-pollinating her flowers
by hand, in case
the bees hadn't done it right.

Her fingertips
sticky and yellow, she touches
my cheek and asks,

Who was the first
person who ever thought to eat
an artichoke?

Inside, I check
to see in her bedroom mirror,
and her golden

buttery thumbprint marks my face,
that blooms alien,
like some pale and questioning flower.

Loneliness

My father made me keep
the bright orange Sanka cans,
with holes in the lids
for ventilation, on
the back porch overnight.
But by morning, sunlight
had steeped my frogs
like tea bags, their bodies
hot to touch as I laid
them out under
the Nanking cherry trees
and tried to revive them
with cold water
from the garden hose.
When my father took
them away to bury,
my mother asked me not
to cry. That night
was the Fourth of July,
and my mother and father
and I went up to the attic
to watch the fireworks,
each with a plate-sized
circle of watermelon.
I remember the rusty smell
of metal and dirt from
the attic screen windows,
which were rarely opened;
how they were littered
with the clear, silver skins
of mayflies, who had shed

the boundaries of their old
bodies so easily. I remember
how silent it was in between
the sporadic, bass-drum putter
and teakettle whistling
of the fireworks, and how,
like some exotic, spangled
night-blooming radiance,
desolation flowered again
and again over the roofs
of our neighbors' houses.

DDT

My parents learned to hear
the hollow crumple of gravel in the alley,
the lumbering hum of

the truck's engine even
in their sleep, and could leap from their bed at predawn—
snapping on all the lights,

storm windows shimmying
down screens to hit bottom with a metallic click,
the outer windows slammed

shut, topped by a squeaky twist
of the lock for good measure. Both former war children,
this was all executed

with the precision of
an air-raid drill—I could hear my mother's bare feet
pat the floor as she moved

from window to window,
calling out, *DDT! DDT! Don't you breathe!*
It frightened me to wake

this way, and I would hold
my breath, squeezing my face deep into the pillow,
sure that a single whiff

would either kill me dead
or instantly transform me into a child of
thalidomide. The well-

planned world my parents mapped
had grown venomous and strange with Charlie Manson,
Kent State, Agent Orange,

LSD. The truck came
by again at dusk, and the neighborhood children
ran behind it—the sweet

spray of the pesticide
cooling the heat and dust from their bodies, settling
on the backs of their tongues

like finely misted sugar
water. And once again, my parents would repeat
their ritual of sealing

shut their house. This is one
of the gestures by which I remember my parents—
locking their windows to

keep me from a world much
too poisonous for their approval, my mother
urging me not to breathe.

I turned out stubborn, head-
strong, and couldn't wait to claw through the window screens,
inhale and be transformed—

like the moths with extra
antennae, or frogs with the multiple limbs of
a Hindu goddess, blind

fish with a third, wide eye.

Dream Carp

People traveled from miles away to see
my paintings of fish—
the jeweled armor of their scales, the beadlike

set of their eyes in
rubbery socket rings, the glimmering
swish of fin and tail

so real it seemed that you could almost dip
a net deep into
the paper and pull up the arching wet

weight of a golden carp,
a shiny trout, or the dark muscular
heft of a bass with

its mouth stretched into the surprised, wiry
"oh" of a child's wind
sock. I captured my models from the sea,

lake, and goldfish pond
in the back garden, so careful not to
let their mouths be torn

by the hook, their scales chipped, or the silky
tissue of their tails
ripped by a clumsy hand. I kept them in

large glass bowls, fed them
mosquito wings or dry silkworm pupas
offered from chopsticks,

and when I was finished making sketches,
I quickly took them
back and set them free again. Every

night I dream I swim
with these fish as a golden carp—black spots
on cloisonné scales,

pulled to the surface by the deceptive
creamy luster of
the moon or the sizzle of firefly lights

across the water.
And every night I am tempted once
again by the smell

of the baited hook, by my predictable
hunger for earthly
things, and each time I am surprised again

by the stinging hook
in my lip that pulls me mercilessly
into the bright air,

setting my gills on fire, the sharp, silver
pain of the knife that
slits me open so easily from tail

to throat to reveal
the scarlet elastic of my raw gills,
the translucent film

of my air sac, the milky rise of my
stomach, and the gray
marbled coil of my intestines. I rise

late each day, and work
in brighter light. When I die, I will
have my paintings brought

down to the lake and slipped into the water.
First the edges of
ink will blur, and then there will be a great

flurry as the fins,
tails, and bodies begin blossoming in-
to life again, each

fish detaching from its canvas of silk
or rice paper—a
swirl of color, motion, swimming away.

Transience

Such a beautiful word, *ephemeroptera*,
for those locust-like convergences
at dusk and at dawn, during the early
days of summer. Storm windows
were opened so the house could breathe
in lilac, which bloomed in voluptuous
fruity clusters—the sweetness
of the scent pierced by a hint
of fresh mint rimming flower
beds on either side of the back door.
One by one, mayflies would arrive
to grip the metal mesh of window
screens in the wiry, tensile crook
of their feet until, from the outside,
the windows appeared to be festooned
with pair after pair of tiny
glistening wings. From inside
my bedroom, the sway-backed curve
of their bodies, slender flourish
of their tail filaments cast shadows
on the insides of my curtains,
and the concentrated gaze of so many
bulging dots of eyes made me feel
as if I were being spied upon.
I was miserable and shy, horribly
in love with a boy who smoked grass
and wore a fading purple jacket.
All summer long a sinewy girl
named Faith, with Breck-girl hair
and a crocheted poncho, met him
behind the band shelter in the park,

where they threw down a blanket
and made out under the lilacs, blue-
jeaned legs tangled, as if trying
to push through the isolation
of their own bodies. Every time
I saw them, I felt as if I were coming
undone, the way a thumbnail splits
open a pea pod, tough green fiber
along the side unzipping the two
halves, the peas inside neatly
spilling out. I stopped riding
my bike and stayed inside, spending
hour after hour watching mayflies
molt on the window screens, the struggle
to pull themselves free from shells
of their old skins. I imagined how
it must have felt to push up
against the margins of the body, that
unforgiving delineation of self,
and feel skin stretching, cracking—
to press the shoulders past itch and hurt,
that triumphant final twist of tail
slithering free, and emerge sleeker,
shinier, brighter, without a mouth
to eat with, exquisite and doomed,
driven to swarm in a mating dance
over water. And what about the boy?
It was so many selves ago, and all
I remember of him now is the lilac
color of that jacket he used to wear.

Happy Hour

I always forget the name,
delphinium,
even though it was the flower

the hummingbirds
loved best. They came in pairs—sleek,
emerald-bright

heads, the clockwork machinery
of their blurred wings
thrumming swift, menacing engines.

They slipped their beaks,
as if they were swizzle sticks, deep
into the blue

throats of delphinium and sucked
dry the nectar-
chilled hearts like goblets full of sweet,

frozen daiquiri.
I liked to sit on the back porch
in the evenings,

watching them and eating Spanish
peanuts, rolling
each nut between thumb and forefinger

to rub away
the red salty skin like brittle
tissue paper,

until the meat emerged gleaming,
yellow like old
ivory, smooth as polished bone.

And late August,
after exclamations of gold
flowers, tiny

and bitter, the caragana
trees let down their
beans to ripen, dry, and rupture—

at first there was
the soft drum of popcorn, slick with oil,
puttering some-

where in between seed, heat, and cloud.
Then sharp cracks like cap
guns or diminutive fireworks,

caragana
peas catapulting skyward like
pellet missiles.

Sometimes a meadowlark would lace
the night air with
its elaborate melody,

rippling and sleek
as a black satin ribbon. Some-
times there would be

a falling star. And because
this happened in
Wyoming, and because this was

my parents' house,
and because I'm never happy
with anything,

at any time, I always wished
that I was some-
where, anywhere else, but here.

Snake Bridegroom

I was helpless
when the soft hairs on the back of my neck
began to stand

up and prickle, and I became aware
that I was not
alone in my bedchamber. I could hear

the *shoji* screen
slide stealthily open and shut, the creak
of the floorboards,

an awful slithering coming closer,
and closer, until
terror spilled open like the explosion

of a bright red
peony in a hailstorm and I knew
that death was near.

And it was precisely at that moment
that my lover
came to me each night to tenderly ease

away my fear
with his cool light touch and the muscular
coil and sinew

of his embrace. He was willow-thin, so
elegant in
pale green robes of the most exquisite silk,

that smelled sweetly,
as if from the scent of freshly crushed leaves.
I could not see

his face in the shadows, but he whispered
strange and lovely
things to me until my eyelids quivered,

slid shut in sleep,
and when I awoke in the morning, he was
already gone.

When my blood stopped flowing with the full moon,
and in the baths
my mother saw how my breasts and belly

were beginning
to swell, my parents called me in to them
and asked me to

reveal the name and family of my
bridegroom. And when
I shamefully admitted that he had

no name, no face,
my mother took me aside and told me
that the next night

I must insert a large embroidery
needle attached
to a spool of thread into the collar

of my lover's
kimono. At first I said I couldn't,
but my mother

coaxed me, and soon desire to see the face
and know the name
of my secret bridegroom overpowered

all of my guilt
over using such a trick to find out
his true nature.

So I did exactly as my mother
instructed me,
and the next morning we followed the length

of thread leading
from my bedroom, tangling through the rice fields,
and unspooling

all the way up to a high mountain cave,
where a dead snake
lay, with jade-green scales and jewel-bright eyes,

his throat cruelly
pierced by the same silver embroidery
needle I pinned

into the collar of my lover's robe
the night before.
I wept, as my mother dragged me away,

and after that,
my thoughts became jumbled and confused. I
imagined that

I could feel my womb twisting and writhing,
full of serpents,
until one day it was too much for me

to bear. I stabbed
myself with a chopstick and set them free
to slither out

where my restless spirit could follow them
through grass and trees,
back up into the mountains, where smooth planes

of rock become
honeyed with the golden heat of sunlight
by mid-morning—

to bask and drench
myself in this yellow sweetness, and dream
again of love.

Octopus in the Freezer

What could you possibly have been dreaming of
as you slumbered coiled there, tentacles
furled about your large soft brow, bashful
and pink, ruminating in the back corner
beneath an arched shelf of antelope ribs—
snugged between headless-bodied broods
of sage grouse, the icy bright pillows
of Shur-Fine lima beans, and the buttered
currency of carrot medallions? What were
you thinking down there in my parents'
basement, blue blood's pulse stilled to a wiry
tangle of navy ribbon, the syncopated bongo-
drum thump and thrum of your three hearts
on break between sets and resting silent
on the stage? By what *unlikelihood*
were you frozen solid in this tightly-wound
pose, like a multi-limbed Hindu goddess
in lotus position, riding the plains by freight
truck to Sakura Square in Denver, where
my mother admired the brawny circumference
of your arms, the snow-white firmness
of your inner flesh, the rubbery erect grip
of your suction cups? And what were the odds
that you'd be packed in dry ice by the *ojii-san*
behind the counter, tucked into our avocado-
green Igloo ice cooler and driven home
across the state line to Wyoming? You remain
frozen in time in my parents' freezer—totemic,
statuesque, infinite and apocryphal—even though
you've been eaten many times over, one arm
at a time, sliced thin into cross-sectioned slivers

for sushi on birthdays and holidays. As a child,
I used to think the dull muffled thud and clunk
of the furnace firing into life at night was the sound
of your head bumping up against the freezer lid,
the cold grate and clash of meats shifting,
scraping against one another in the wake
of your thrashing tentacles' lash and whip.
What error in judgment took you from your cozy
niche, your eclectic garden arranged with such
compulsive precision: the slender-necked
and lush-hipped wine bottles, the shiny winking
bits of mirror startling back your placid mild eye,
the pickle jar whose lid you loved to screw
and unscrew—dangling in a tapered arm,
your exquisitely sensitive, ganglia-rimmed
suckers quivering, to check for tasty things
to eat? Did you become snarled in a fisherman's
net, or clasped tight in the steel embrace
of a lobster trap—caught in the careless
kleptomania of your endless lust for crustacea?
And did your chromatophores pulse first white,
then red, to semaphore the blushing flush
of fear flaming to anger? Were you caped
in a smoky swirl of spewed blackness dispersing
the way *sumi-é* ink curls away from
the tornado whirl of a horsehair brush
being twirled clean in water? Today the snow
just falls and falls, and I think of you
as the relentless volatile wind lifts the flakes
into blinding, shimmering white veils that spiral
and mist—so cold the fine spray delicately
burns for one moment against the skin,
and frozen feathery etchings are flung up
against the windows like splayed bits
of goosedown. Cars and trucks cough and come

to a halt, my back door freezes shut.
The barometer drops and empty wine bottles
line the kitchen counter like bowling pins.
How odd, I keep thinking to myself
as everything around me creaks and groans
and shivers, then stills to ice and frost.
How odd that it has all come to this.
And then I wish for someone, anyone at all,
to dream of me, if only for a moment,
to unfurl my rigid aching limbs and melt down
all my hearts, taste my salt on their tongue,
let ice transubstantiate to breathing flesh,
and resurrect me back into the living again.

Antelope Jerky

That smell, something like wet dog, stayed
on our hands days
after skinning the gutted meat

shell of hollowed-
out antelope on the back lawn—
alternately

shearing through the opaque membrane
of fat that held
skin to flesh with a hunting knife,

or pulling off
larger sections of hide by punching
down with a clenched

fist to reveal the cool smooth lengths
of sinewy
purple meat. Finally, the hooves

and head were sawed
off, my father performing a sort
of craniotomy

to salvage the pronghorn antlers,
boyish and pleased.
On the mountains, quaking aspens

were beginning
to turn, and the chill settling in
as the porch light

was turned on had the precision
edge to etch out
lacy frost flowers overnight

on the window
panes. Our fingers ached underneath
the garden hose

as we rinsed off knives, gristly bits
of grainy bone
caught in the saw's teeth. The next day

my mother honed
her fierce cleaver, long boning knives,
stainless steel shears,

and butchered the antelope one
limb at a time,
my father performing tidy

amputations
in the garage and bringing in
a new section

when my mother called him to say
she was ready.
The meat was carved into steaks, chunked

into stew meat—
slivers and odd bits tossed into
a metal bowl

for jerky. My mother neatly
wrapped everything
in freezer paper and labeled

the packages
in Japanese with black magic
marker, English

translations underneath to be
polite. There was
a special jerky recipe—

brown sugar, soy
sauce, black pepper and Worcestershire,
onion powder.

The leftover meat was fashioned
into slitted
strips, marinated overnight,

then hung in rows
over the wire oven racks. Low
heat for a day,

the house smoky, warm fragrance of
teriyaki,
everyone so impatient

to taste—that same
jerky still in storage today
in my parents'

basement, in Rubbermaid bins,
layered in snug
wax-paper rows, briny and hard

as rock, a kind
of *memento mori* in case of blizzards,
the meat having

now long outlived the antelope.
I remember
one year my mother sliced open

her thumb, was rushed
to the hospital for stitches,
a tetanus shot.

That doctor, he was so surprised
I was cutting
up an antelope, my mother

said later with
a strange kind of pride as she held
up her thumb, bruised

and swollen, the black ends of thread
from the stitches
wiry and poking up like twisted

insect legs—her
tiny thumb that, although without
the hook of purple

scar to interrupt the sig-
nature print's swirl
and whorl, I see with a startling

flash is the same
thumb that I now wear on my own
hand, my very own.

Transplanting

For my mother, Yoshiko Horikoshi Roripaugh

1. X-Ray

My mother carried the chest x-ray
in her lap on the plane, inside
a manila envelope that read
Do Not Bend and, garnished
with leis at the Honolulu Airport,
waited in line—this strange image
of ribcage, chain-link vertebrae,
pearled milk of lung, and the murky
enigmatic chambers of her heart
in hand. Until it was her turn
and the immigration officer held
the black-and-white film up
to sun, light pierced clean through
her, and she was ushered from one
life through the gate of another,
wreathed in the dubious and illusory
perfume of plucked orchids.

2. *Ceramic Pig*

Newly arrived in New Mexico,
stiff and crisp in new dungarees,
her honeymoon, they drove
into the mountains in a borrowed car,
spiraling up and up toward the rumor
of deer, into the green tangy turpentine

scent of pine, where air crackled
with the sizzling collision of bees,
furred legs grappling velvet bodies
as they mated midair, and where
they came upon the disconsolate gaze
of a Madonna alcoved against
the side of the road, her feet wreathed
in candles, fruit, flowers, and other
offerings. Nearby, a vendor
with a wooden plank balanced between
two folding chairs and the glossy
row of ceramic pigs lined up across,
brilliant glaze shimmering the heat.
My mother fell in love with the red-
and-blue splash of flowers tattooed
into fat flanks and bellies, the green
arabesques of stem and leaf circling
hoof, snout, and ear. *So exotic.*
Years later she still describes the pig
with a sigh—*heartbroken,* the word
she chooses with careful consideration.
She'd filled the pig with Kennedy dollars
from the grocery budget, each half dollar
a small luxury denied at the local
Piggly Wiggly, until one day, jingling
the shift and clink of the pig's
growing silver weight, she shook
too hard, and as if the hoarded wealth
of her future were too much to contain,
the pig broke open—spilling coins
like water, a cold shiny music, into her lap—
fragments of bright pottery shards
scattering delicate as Easter eggshell.

3. *Sneeze*

My mother sneezes in Japanese. *Ké-sho!*
An exclamation of surprise—two sharp
crisp syllables before pulling out
the neatly folded and quartered tissue
she keeps tucked inside the wrist
of her sweater sleeve. Sometimes,
when ragweed blooms, I wonder why
her sneeze isn't mine, why something
so involuntary, so deeply rooted
in the seed of speech, breaks free from
my mouth like thistle in a stiff breeze,
in a language other than my mother's
tongue. How do you chart the diaspora
of a sneeze? *I don't know how*
you turned out this way, she always
tells me, and I think that we are each
her own moon—one face in shadow,
undisclosed seas and surprising mountains,
rotating in the circular music
of separate spheres, but held in orbit
by the gravitational muscle
of the same mercurial spinning heart.

4. *Dalmatian*

There is an art to this. To shish
kebab the varnished pit of avocado
on three toothpicks above a pickle jar
of cool water, tease down the pale
thirsty hairs of root until one sinewy
arm punches up and unclenches its green
fisted hand, palm open, to the sun.

To discern the oniony star-struck
subterfuge of bulbs, their perverse
desires, death-like sleeps, and conspire
behind the scenes to embroider
the Elizabethan ruffles and festoons
of their flamboyant resurrections.
To trick the tomatoes into letting down
their swelling, tumescent orbs
in the cottony baked heat of the attic
until their sunburnt faces glow
like round orange lanterns under
the crepuscular twilight of the eaves.
Unwrapping the cuttings of succulents
from their moist, paper-towel bandages,
and snugging them down into firm
dimples of dirt and peat, coaxing up
the apple-green serpentine coils of sweet
pea with a snake charmer's song to wind
around the trellis and flicker their quick
pink-petaled tongues. The tender slips
of mint, sueded upturned bells of petunia,
and slim fingers of pine that pluck
the metal window screen like a tin harp
by the breakfast nook where my father
stirs his morning coffee and waits
for the neighbors' Dalmatian to hurl
itself over the back fence and hang,
limply twisting and gasping on the end
of its chain and collar like a polka-dotted
petticoat, until my father goes outside
and takes its baleful kicking weight
in his arms and gently tosses it back
over the fence into the neighbors' yard.
Year after year, the dandelions

and clover are weeded out, summers
come and go, and roots stubbornly inch
down around the foundation of the house—
labyrinthine, powerful and deep.

5. *Japanese Apple*

She was given an apple on the plane,
round and fragrant with the scent
of her grandfather's fruit orchards
during autumn, when chestnuts
dropped from their trees and struck
the metal rooftop like the small heavy
tongues of bells, and black dragon-
flies like quick shiny needles darted
in and out of the spin and turn
of leaves fluttering down like soft
bright scraps of silk. She wrapped
the apple in a napkin to save
for later, and it was confiscated
at customs before she had the chance
for even a taste. Over the years it
seemed to grow larger, yellower, juicier
and more delicious, and even though
there were burnished rows of apples
stacked in gleaming pyramids
at the supermarket with quaint
names like Macintosh, Winesap,
and Granny Smith, and even though
there were sunlit apple orchards
at my American grandfather's ranch,
where rattlesnakes slumbered
in the heat and redolence of fruit
flesh, frightening the horses,

she sampled one after another,
but they never tasted as sweet
or as bright as the apple taken from her,
the one she had to leave behind.

Nanking Cherry Jam

The robins squabbled over the berries
late in the summer
when they began to ferment—slick bruised

pulp intoxicating the birds into
a raucous frenzy.
Sometimes one would break into crooked flight,

become confused and crash into the clear,
shining expanse of
the porch-room window. Knocked out cold, toothpick

legs stabbing the air, its orange paunch was
incongruous among
the slender limbs of iris, who unfurled

their yellow-striped tongues and lifted their frilled
wrists up to assume
the statuesque poses of flamenco

dancers. Each time a robin was fallen,
my mother sat guard
on the back porch, poised with a garden hose,

waiting to spray any cat who came by
looking to snatch up
a non-confrontational meal. But wait.

I've almost forgotten all about
the cherry blossoms.
How they began as tight green buds the size

of glass pinheads, then erupted almost
overnight like strings
of popcorn—puffy and white, with a faint

pink blush. A tiny bird, not a sparrow,
would come to nibble
at the petals. After a while, they'd begin to loosen

themselves from their moorings of stem, bud, branch,
carried by the breeze
so that it was almost a winter blizzard

again outside the dining-room windows,
except for the heat,
the lazy, sweet pink haze of fragrance that

hypnotized the bumblebees, fat and furred,
who came to rumble
their deep-throated purr into the sticky waxed

ears of flowers. I thought my mother seemed
happier in the
company of cherry blossoms. She used

to say that once you leave a place, it's best
not to be always
looking over your own shoulder, but I

don't see how this could be true. I remember
the taste of the jam
she used to make from the Nanking cherries.

Underneath the milky paraffin cap,
not quite the color
of garnets, but more pink, like rhodolites,

we spread it in sticky clumps over warm
yellow squares of corn-
bread, or across wedges of morning toast—

and though the jam was always bittersweet
against my tongue,
I still could taste the fragrant blood-red fruit.

Instinct

Bottle rockets and beer,
my eyes sting
and I wander from
my friends' smoky chatter.
Do they know my heart's
gone wrong again?
Night's heat stifles me
like an unwanted kiss
and something intangible
sprouts fingers.
I find a luna moth.
She quivers in the water,
large as the palm
of my hand, black
circles like eyes. I lift
her out with a pool net,
the papier-mâché body
tangled in damp mesh.
Prickly legs grip
my fingers, antennae
question the breath I blow
across chlorined wings.

All that afternoon
we'd fished tree frogs
out to keep them
from dismemberment
in the ruthless suck
and thrum of the pool's
vacuum. Slippery, muscled
bodies emerald bright,

their bulbous fingers
were sticky and clever—
swivel of gleaming,
prehistoric eye and tender
palpitating bellies.
We slipped them into
Tupperware and Rubbermaid
and carried them down
to the sliver of creek
to let them go—jeweled
heads beating the lids
like microwave popcorn.
Hours later, they were back,
cool mossy bumps with songs
too big for their bodies
lining the undersides
of the pool gutters.

I don't know what it is
that brings me
to this same point, time
after time. Maybe my spirit
is inconsolable
the same way this luna moth,
who navigates by the light
of the sun and the moon,
was mistakenly drawn in
by the pool's flood lamps.
But I make too much
of this moth, waiting
for her to die in my hands.
Fireworks, mosquitoes
raising welts on my back,
fingers mushrooming

the poison home. And when
the quivering stops,
I make myself crush it,
like a cigarette butt
underneath my shoe.

Girl with a Bowl on Her Head

When I was a girl, my mother
always made me

wear a wooden bowl on my head.
She wanted to

keep people from looking at me
and it worked. No

one ever really saw me, but
only the bowl,

or what they thought they might have glimpsed
concealed below,

and soon I became secretive
as an acorn.

I cultivated a new way
of seeing and

became a connoisseur of strange,
vegetal things

kept hidden inside—the second
miniature

bell pepper nested inside the first
like a Russian

doll, green, with the intricate curl
and fold of an

ear. Or how the inscrutable
placid carrot

ripening into anarchy
splits wide open

and bares its ropey length of barbed,
thorny spine. Or

the tearing apart of spicy
cool globes of or-

anges to sometimes find an extra
section, the size

of a lima bean, tucked between
two large sections

like a flower pressed in the pages
of a thick book.

Hungrily picking and plucking
at the thistled

leaves of an artichoke, down to
the translucent

purple-tipped petals that flutter
thin as gills, down

past the nest of buttery fur
cropped close like a

scrub brush that comes off in sticky
clumps, all the way

down to the green, sweet creamy heart.

Ennui

Sometimes I feel I'm on an island
in the lake of lost connections,
where insects buzz and hum
their electric song,
and the metronomical blink
of the cursor's eye is a beacon
to the shore beyond. I keep
starting and restarting letters
to people I once knew, but I feel
brittle and strange, and can't find
the right words, or at least
the ones I need. Autumn tightens
its crisp band of air like a tourniquet,
and the man-size sunflower across
the alleyway from my back door
dries on its stalk and becomes
a ghost. The cats sleep closer
now that it is cool, their bodies
heavy and round, the oddity
of their cat thoughts self-contained.
In the morning on the bus
I see the same woman every day
outside the Shell station, wheeling
her grocery cart that holds only
a green street sign reading "Emily Way";
and the man who clasps a plum-
colored Igloo lunch cooler
with such formality, chest level,
using both hands palms up, as if
offering up his own heart. I wear

my anonymity like a scar and consider
it an excuse for voyeurism.

On the way home, behind the coffee
shop, I pass the skeleton of a sparrow,
licked clean over the course of a week
by clusters of black ants, whose
nervous, rippling activity reminded
me of television static. Now
the bare, delicate architecture
of the bird is almost fetal—tiny
skull compact as a cowry shell,
the empty curl of the ribcage,
the vertebrae of the spine linked
together with the intricate precision
of an expensive bracelet.

All evening long I keep checking
on the praying mantis
who came to perch on the lid
of the trash can. I am lost
between one thing and another,
and can't remember which. Absinthe
green, with its backwards-pointing
knees rising in stiff peaks,
it swivels around its triangular wedge
of a head to gaze at me
with black pinpoints of eyes
each time I step out my back door
onto the stoop, and it seems as if
she is saying to me, *Have you ever
eaten a pomegranate?* I buy one
from the Big Bear grocery
on the corner, and the seeds
are brilliant, clear as rubies nested

in the fleshy concave hollows
of pulp. And as I pluck them out
one by one to eat, each one
leaves behind an emptiness, each
one making me more a thief.

Tongue-Cut Sparrow

Once I was a sparrow
caught trespassing in your back garden
and you made me your pet,

feeding me satin seeds of tear-shaped
sesame from the tip
of your finger, blowing your warm breath

in the tender hollows
beneath the curve of my wings. You tried
to keep me hidden in

the sleeve of your kimono, but none-
theless, when your back was
turned, your wife snatched me up and cut out

my tongue with gardening
shears—the hot, sudden taste of rust, blood
and silence blossoming

in my mouth like a red peony.
A sparrow silenced by
a wife will become a woman of

delicately-coded
gestures—one who uses her body to sing,
and can uncurl her wrist

in a certain way so that her hand
blooms like an azalea,
or bows her head as she looks away

so that the nape of her
neck is revealed and the fine silk hairs
stir like dandelion

seeds. A woman like this can make a man
leave his wife and follow
her anywhere, and so I led you

through a maze of bookshops,
coffeehouses and nightclubs, and let
you watch me dance. I pre-

tended that you were mine for awhile,
until your wife found us
and took you home. As you were leaving,

I gave you a box filled
with freshwater pearls, slippery to touch,
and green like the color

of tea. You traded them all to buy
your wife a noodle shop, and
a week later, you returned to me.

Maybe your wife had sent
you to bring back another, larger
box, or maybe, like me,

she was beginning to find that you
were not worth all this trouble.
So I gave you another box—this

one much more beautiful
on the outside than the first, but crammed
full of sparrows' tongues, mouse

droppings, and pure-white poisonous snakes.
I grew a new, tough tongue,
and finally set myself free.

Nostalgia

Yellow monarchs came
to sample the sweet William
from my mother's garden
and my father taught me
to charm them—
how to creep up on one,
keeping the startling edges
of my shadow concealed,
the offer of my index finger,
branch-like. I'd hold
my breath and wait, dizzy
in that heart-stopping
moment when a butterfly
would test the strange
terrain of my skin in
the delicate pincer grip
of its feet. Sometimes
I would pluck off a sprig
of sweet William so that
I could see it unfurl
the black wiry length
of its sinewy tongue,
which was wrapped
with the tight precision
of a roll of licorice,
and slip it down, clever
as a coat hanger,
to unlock the heart
of the flower's sweetness.
But it was always
the monarch caterpillars

I loved best—their juicy
ripe-fruit plumpness,
shocking school-bus yellow
and elaborate tattoo
of their talcum-powder skin;
the slinky give and take
on lovely, suction-cup feet.
I kept them as pets, fed
them Swiss chard and lettuce.
It was the *before* of them
I loved—before the obsessed
thread spinning, the chill
and shroud of the cocoon, before
the need to completely
recreate themselves into
a winged scaled thing
with an unappeasable hunger
and unknown miles to go.

Snake Wife

From the very start, you were charmed
by the uncoiling
languor of my shifting poses,

by the sibilant
lisp of silk sliding down my un-
dulant length of spine

as I shed the intricate layers
of my kimono
one by one—first, the sun-colored

overcoat, and then
the brocaded gown embroidered
with the pattern of

falling maple leaves, clear down to
the delicate white
folds of the innermost lining.

Outside, the slender
bodies of black dragonflies, with
their flashing velvet

wings, stitched together the swirling
yellow leaves like quick
black darning needles, while I kept

you hypnotized by
my unblinking gaze glittering
from beneath the sheer

film of brille, the cool sinuous
ripple of smoothly
oiled skin, and the haunting flicker

of my forked tongue. You
allowed yourself to see only
those things you wished me

to be, and because I loved you,
I let you go on
this way, learning to veil myself

in self-deception—
soon gaining a reputation
as a woman of

exquisite refinement because
my modesty was
such it prevented anyone

from more than fleeting
glimpses behind the hand-painted
silk fans I fluttered

in front of my face in the same way
that butterfly wings
open and shut (open and shut)

on the tiniest
of hinges. And strangely enough,
I even became

known as a great beauty. Before
the start of winter
my belly first began to stir

and swell with the fruit
of our autumnal lovemaking,
and by the time of

the rainy season, water spilled
from between my legs
and I was seized by an awful,

white-hot pain. You made
me a promise not to look
inside the birth room,

no matter what unnatural
or unearthly sound
you heard from behind the *shoji*

screen. But in the end,
curiosity was larger
than your love for me,

and so you cut a notch into
the rice paper just
large enough to fit one prying

eye, and then you cried
out in shock—there was a baby,
our infant son, coiled

in the grasp of a giant white
snake, and shining gold
pieces of eggshell scattered in

splendor all throughout
the room. And because you had seen
me as my true self,

I plucked out one of my own eyes
to give to our child
to suckle, and then I left you.

I have always been
too proud in this way. But you were
irresponsible,

and let the eye fall down a well,
forcing me to come
back and pluck out the other eye

when I heard my child's
hungry cries. Now I thread my way
through life on instinct,

and by the shifting and subtle
flavors of the air
caressed by my flickering tongue.

And oh, how I wish
sometimes that I were a white fox,
or a golden koi,

or the long elegant crane that winters
in snow country by
the hot springs where macaques linger

and bathe—red faces
bright in snow and steam, grooming each
other with soft paws.

Albino Squirrel

Pumpkin after pumpkin crumples into the rows
of front porches, lopsided faces like stroke
victims, and it is the time of year when I avoid
their drooping gaze because I, too,
feel disconsolate—scooped out and overblown
with too much ripeness. Maple leaves palm
the wet sidewalk with red, splayed fingers
as if to keep the mold and damp from rising,
and my mind stretches taut as the lines of web
that spiders pluck and tap with bent, clever legs—
their nimble pizzicato a Morse code of desire
and fear. Last night a possum bared its teeth
to me and hissed from the corner of my back porch
where it crouched, all shiny tin-foil eyes
and terse, bald pink tail when I surprised
its meticulous inventory of the neighbors' trash.
Each time I tried to sneak out to the dumpster,
ridiculous, armed with a broom in one hand,
a Big Bear bag full of cat poop in the other,
it was still there, crouching, nocturnal
and vigilant, hiss spiraling into a growl. I left it
and went to bed where my lover cocooned
in the brown tick and hum of the electric blanket,
tightly rolled and snug as an enchilada—oblivious
to my attempts to unwrap her, to the shift
and held-breath tension of the bed as I hunched
into my own, separate blanket and touched myself.
Delicate flickering to ease down the slick,
fragrant warmth until everything was satin, swollen
ripe fruit, and desire uncoiled its heavy braid
in dull, furtive pulse beats. Sometimes it seems

as if there is no warning, not even a slender
line of thread whose vibrations I can decode,
and I woke in the morning desiccated and numb,
tangled in bedclothes. On the way to the bus stop,
toward the certainty of another day measured
in tea bags, timesheets, the endless bony click
and clatter of computer keys—a day I know
will fade as easily as regret—I am startled by
leaves hitting asphalt as they plummet from trees.
I can't help thinking this must be like the sound
of all those butterflies sprayed with insecticide
at the end of the summer exhibit, cascading
onto the conservatory floor—the soft, brittle rain
of color, motion suddenly stopped. I've carried
this peculiar sorrow in my heart as if it were
a sparrow in a cage, and on mornings like this
I can feel it swell its breast, puffing out feathers
against the chill. I see an albino squirrel weaving
its way through the rush-hour line of cars,
leaping onto the sidewalk to pause in front
of me—like white velvet, with sleek muscular
haunches, a glamorous plume of tail. Red
jeweled eyes glittered like pomegranate seeds,
and he gripped an enormous acorn in his mouth
as if it were everything—carrying it toward
the promise of his well-lined nest, toward warmth
and sleep, the solitary ambrosia of oblivion.

Toothpick Warriors

Night sweats
to the rattle
and clink
of their armor—
marching grooves
around my bed,
pulling toothpicks
from *tatami*
to disembowel
each other,
or skewer
and roast
a beetle, fine
bone china
of their saké cups
rolling the sound
of marbles
when they drop them
on the hard-
wood floors at dawn.

You think
I'm making this up
but they never
liked you anyway
and you are less
than flesh,
more a ghost—
quick and sweet
as opium smoke,
indelible

as the curl of red
unfurling
into the syringe
before exploding
poppy-bright
into fire
and backdraft,
until everything
blazes gold
and heat,
like the memory
of Mishima's
golden pavilion
resurrected
into flame.

Stay and watch.
I can make them
afraid of me.
Here is the white
linen headband
I wrap around
your forehead.
Here is perfumed
cotton wool
I use to pack
your anus.
This is the dagger
I unwind from silk
to hand to you.
And here the sword
I'll use to cleave
delusion's head
clean off.

Hope

There are nights I dream of goldfish,
and in my dreams they sing to me in
fluted, piercing sopranos like the Vienna
Boys Choir. Although in the daylight
they are mostly silent and ravenous—
the suction-cup grip of their mouths
on my fingertip like tiny rubber bath-
room plungers when they rise to strike
at an offering of chopped green peas.
Sometimes a frenetic clicking of marbles
nosed and nudged across the aquarium
floor during scavenging sessions for food,
sounding like the rack and crack of a game
of pool. Such hunger. Such extravagance.

Their ovoid bodies are like Faberge eggs
filigreed with flakes of hammered gold,
a glittering armor of polished gill
plates, their dorsal fins elegant ribbed
silk fans that open when in motion,
and fold themselves shut in repose.
Clever pectoral fins maneuver and oscillate
like small propellers, and the circling
tails flare and twirl with the hypnotic
flourish of the toreador's cape. All
is endless metaphor here. All of it.

I once read the goldfish memory span
was three seconds, and does this mean
each moment is an astonishment

in a series of quick incarnations spiraling
outward the way water ripples away
from a disturbance, so that, in the end,
each brief flicker of awareness
is long enough to learn to simply *be,*
and isn't this really, after all, enough?

One morning I woke to find the red-capped
oranda in distress—fins clamped sadly
down, listless tail, gasping on the back
corner floor of the aquarium. I netted
her and put her in a glass bowl sugared
with a quarter cup of sea salt crystals—
the way my Japanese grandfather once
showed my mother, and the way my mother,
years later in America, once showed me.

And several hours later, the sheer veils
of tail and fin began to bloom, to resume
their arabesques and veronicas around
the sleek shimmer of her white satin body—
the scandal of her scarlet cap dipping
coquettishly, onyx beads of eyes swiveling
in their turquoise socket rings. She swam
around and around the clear glass bowl,
until my heart swung left and followed her
around and around from above the way
red-throated loons on the Island of Seto
circle and follow the fishing boats, tamed
by the fishermen, and calling out
with their strange and mournful cries.

White Butterfly

The cicadas are shy and hard to find
tonight, as always,
even though their music is tangible,

like heat. It presses
shrill and strong against the skin, pulls me up-
right, and makes my pulse

flower again. Red dragonflies slither
free from molted shells,
roll enormous glittering eyes and lick

their glistening tails.
The bola spider will pull a single
line of silk from her

round creamy-orange bottom—she jewels it
with beads of perfume
that smell like the musk of a female moth,

and then swings her thread
like a bright pearl lasso above her head
until a male moth,

brave with lust, flies into the spiral snare
of her twirling rope
and is wrapped quick and neat as a fatted

calf. And when the time
has come for you to close your eyes and shed
your shell of muscle,

blood, and bone, I'll come to you in the form
of a white butter-
fly. I'll ride in on the back of a black

dragonfly with wings
laced as intricately as a Spanish
mantilla, and when

breath becomes lonely in the bare dusky
chamber of your rib
cage, I will flutter above the cool void

of your mouth, uncurl
the sinewy, incense-like coil of my
tongue and reach deep in-

side you, as if you were honeysuckle,
rescue your last breath
from the brittle carapace of your

body, and then fan
it with swift powerful beats of my wings
until it opens

up and breaks free—the way the cloudy heads
of dandelions
gone to seed escape the green anchors of

their stems. Then you can
drift past the purple borders of cosmos,
red Gerber daisies

with their velvet plush-button centers, the white
and yellow spicy
points of chrysanthemums in your garden,

past the grave of the
woman I used to be, which you tended
for so many years,

to the river where rice paper lanterns
will spill their yellow
glow onto the water like bright splashes

of pottery glaze
as they are set into the slow, deep pull
of the current to

float downstream during *obon*—the chain
of light unfolding
and uncoiling like a shimmering gold

serpent. Remember
the memory of this light and follow it
wherever it leads

you, because you are all spirit, breath, and
seed now. I will come
with you and show you. I will take you home.

Other Books in the Crab Orchard Award Series in Poetry

Muse
Susan Aizenberg

Millennial Teeth
Dan Albergotti

Hijra
Hala Alyan

*Instructions, Abject
& Fuming*
Julianna Baggott

*Lizzie Borden in Love:
Poems in Women's
Voices*
Julianna Baggott

This Country of Mothers
Julianna Baggott

The Black Ocean
Brian Barker

Vanishing Acts
Brian Barker

Objects of Hunger
E. C. Belli

*Nostalgia for a World
Where We Can Live*
Monica Berlin

The Sphere of Birds
Ciaran Berry

White Summer
Joelle Biele

Gold Bee
Bruce Bond

Rookery
Traci Brimhall

USA-1000
Sass Brown

*The Gospel according
to Wild Indigo*
Cyrus Cassells

*In Search of the Great
Dead*
Richard Cecil

*Twenty First Century
Blues*
Richard Cecil

Circle
Victoria Chang

Errata
Lisa Fay Coutley

Salt Moon
Noel Crook

Consolation Miracle
Chad Davidson

From the Fire Hills
Chad Davidson

The Last Predicta
Chad Davidson

Unearth
Chad Davidson

Furious Lullaby
Oliver de la Paz

Names above Houses
Oliver de la Paz

Dots & Dashes
Jehanne Dubrow

*The Star-Spangled
Banner*
Denise Duhamel

Smith Blue
Camille T. Dungy

Seam
Tarfia Faizullah

Beautiful Trouble
Amy Fleury

Sympathetic Magic
Amy Fleury

Egg Island Almanac
Brendan Galvin

Soluble Fish
Mary Jo Firth Gillett

Pelican Tracks
Elton Glaser

Winter Amnesties
Elton Glaser

Strange Land
Todd Hearon

View from True North
Sara Henning

Always Danger
David Hernandez

Heavenly Bodies
Cynthia Huntington

Terra Nova
Cynthia Huntington

*Maps for Migrants
and Ghosts*
Luisa A. Igloria